Made in the USA
Monee, IL
01 May 2021

67425058R00065